Sketching Outdoors in Summer

— Summer Visitor —
turkey vultures
as they circled low
over my head

J W Arnosky
July 16, 1987

ALSO BY JIM ARNOSKY

Deer at the Brook

Drawing from Nature

Drawing Life in Motion

Flies in the Water, Fish in the Air:
A Personal Introduction to Fly Fishing

Freshwater Fish & Fishing

Gray Boy

Raccoons and Ripe Corn

Secrets of a Wildlife Watcher

Sketching Outdoors in Spring

Watching Foxes

LOTHROP, LEE & SHEPARD BOOKS   NEW YORK

Sketching Outdoors in Summer

BY JIM ARNOSKY

First Edition   1   2   3   4   5   6   7   8   9   10

Library of Congress Cataloging in Publication Data
Arnosky, Jim   Sketching outdoors in summer.
Summary: Provides drawings of landscapes, plants, animals, and other aspects of nature, accompanied by comments from the artist on how and why he drew them.
1. Outdoor life in art—Juvenile literature. 2. Animals in art—Juvenile literature. 3. Plants in art—Juvenile literature. 4. Wildlife art—Juvenile literature.
5. Landscape in art—Juvenile literature. 6. Summer in art—Juvenile literature. 7. Drawing—Technique—Juvenile literature. [1. Nature (Aesthetics)
2. Landscape drawing—Technique. 3. Animal painting and illustration—Technique. 4. Drawing—Techniques]
. Title.   NC825.088A78   1988   743'.83   87-29728   ISBN 00-688-06286-5

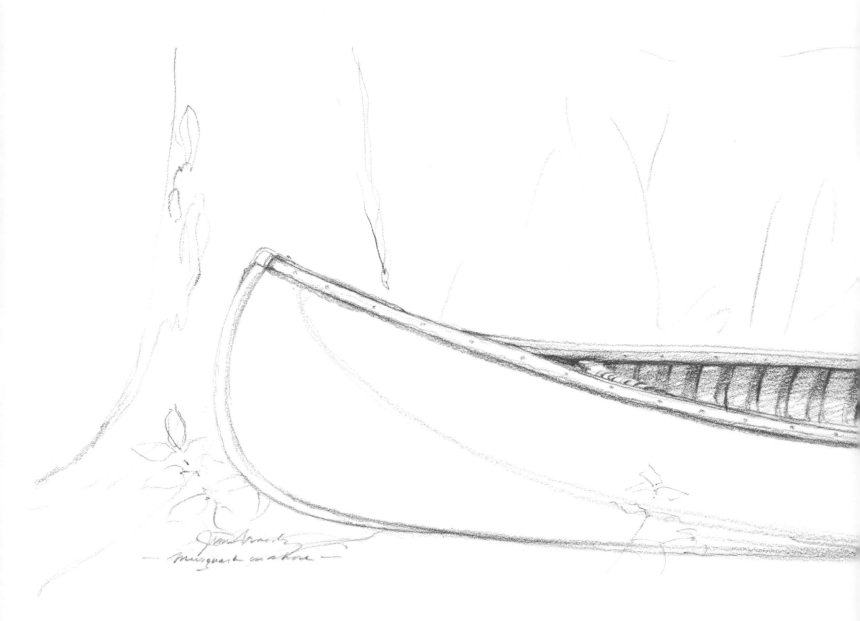

This book is dedicated to Deanna.
Summer is her season. She sows its promise
in the garden rows, cultivates its beauty in the
flower beds, and spreads its warmth
with her smile.

MUSQUASH II

INTRODUCTION

"What pleasant paths begin in gardens . . ."
Henry Beston

I began sketching summer in our garden, at the base of an old and rotting tree on which three bird boxes hang. From the garden the pleasant path of my summer sketching meandered through the yard and around the house, then wandered off to nearby meadows and fields. Because I am a fisherman, all my paths eventually lead to water. I made sketches by the river, along the banks of trout ponds, and on the waters of big lakes.

A number of the sketches were done while summer showers soaked my paper, pencil lines, and me. The raindrops felt refreshing after my work in the hot summer sun.

To protect my skin from the sun, I used sun-blocking lotion, especially on my nose and cheeks. Sunlight reflects brightly off the surface of drawing paper; to protect my eyes from the reflected light, I wore dark glasses with polarizing lenses. I sometimes sat under an umbrella. Most of the time, however, a wide-brimmed hat sufficed for shade. Even with all these precautions, my skin was browned and my moustache bleached.

Though biting insects were not a problem while I was outdoors sketching, I carried repellent just in case I encountered a swarm of black flies or mosquitos and found myself the center of their attention.

These summer sketches are about things I love doing, as well as things I enjoy drawing. They show our busy little farm. They take you to other places where I spend summer time. Some are secret spots. The paths leading to them are mine alone. It is my hope that this book will start you on a path of your own— sketching outdoors in summer.

Jim Arnosky
Ramtails
Summer 1987

HERE IS THE NEST-BOX TREE at the edge of our garden. Ten summers ago, after cutting some hay, I hung my scythe on the nest-box tree. I haven't cut hay since. The scythe still hangs there. Its long curving handle has turned the same weathered gray as the dead tree's trunk. Birds perch below on the scythe's handgrip and above on its rusting blade.

I was sketching the scythe and the bird boxes all hanging on the tree when a pair of bluebirds alighted nearby, up on the telephone wire. The birds carried insects in their beaks. They stayed on the wire, fidgeting impatiently. I understood and walked some distance away. Then, one at a time, they flew down to their nesting box and fed their young. I could hear the baby birds chirping excitedly inside the box.

This is a perfect subject to begin a season's sketching! There is just enough light, shadow, construction, shape, and texture to engage the hand without overwhelming the mind.

When sketching, choose the parts of your subject you wish to feature. Detail and shade only those areas. Leave in light outline parts that are important to your picture's composition but are not its main focus of interest.

The bluebird on the wire was sketched from life. The bluebird at the nest box was drawn from a fresh recollection only minutes after the actual sight. Train your mind to freeze and retain images of moving bodies.

A Box of Bluebirds
June 23, 1987

Fantails in Summer after two days rain —

Jim Arnosky
June 27/28
1987

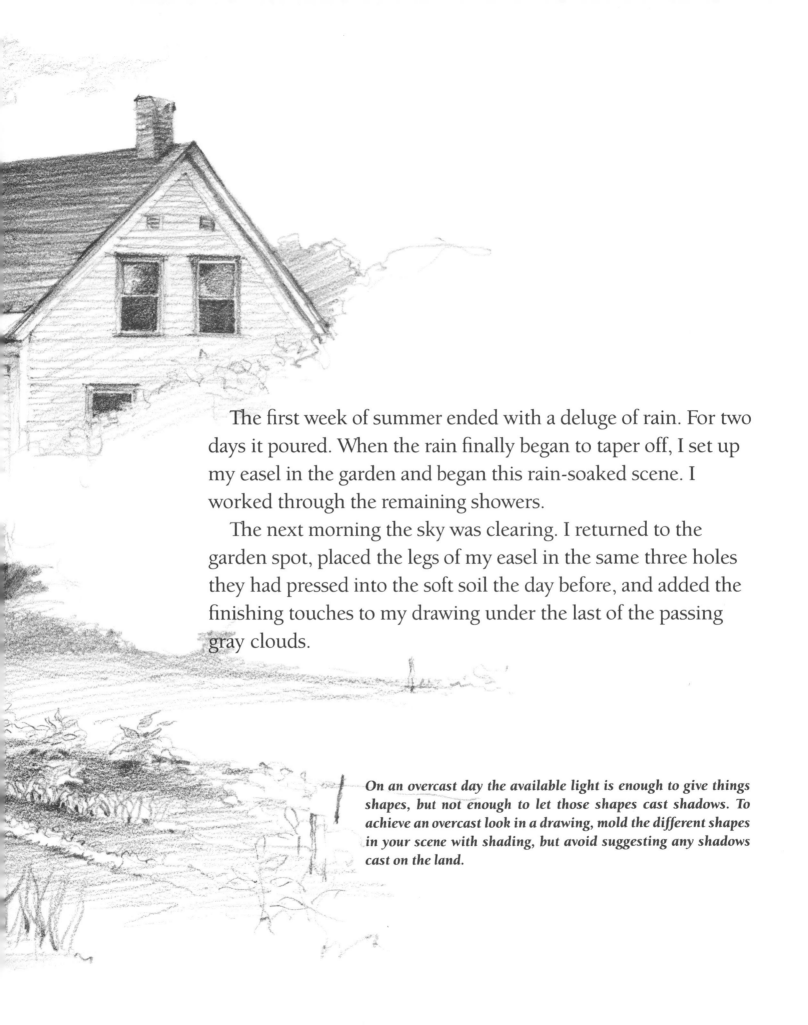

The first week of summer ended with a deluge of rain. For two days it poured. When the rain finally began to taper off, I set up my easel in the garden and began this rain-soaked scene. I worked through the remaining showers.

The next morning the sky was clearing. I returned to the garden spot, placed the legs of my easel in the same three holes they had pressed into the soft soil the day before, and added the finishing touches to my drawing under the last of the passing gray clouds.

On an overcast day the available light is enough to give things shapes, but not enough to let those shapes cast shadows. To achieve an overcast look in a drawing, mold the different shapes in your scene with shading, but avoid suggesting any shadows cast on the land.

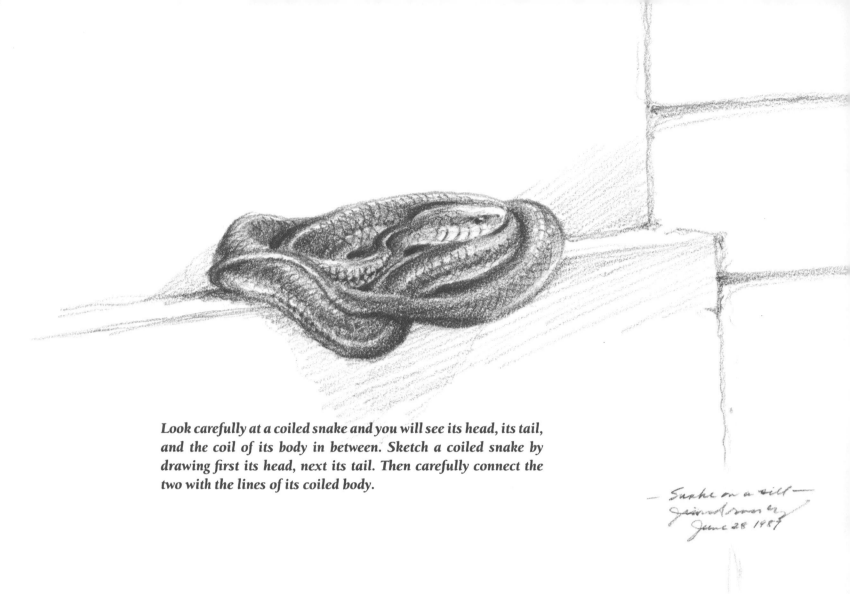

Look carefully at a coiled snake and you will see its head, its tail, and the coil of its body in between. Sketch a coiled snake by drawing first its head, next its tail. Then carefully connect the two with the lines of its coiled body.

Snake on a sill
Jim Arnosky
June 28 1987

Deanna discovered this garter snake on the house. It had climbed the clapboard siding and was warming itself on a sunlit sill. The drawing shows the snake's actual size. Look how it has coiled on such a narrow space.

On the opposite page is another snake, one I spotted as it moved through a flowerbed. When the snake noticed me, it froze with its head held a few inches off the ground. The snake stayed that way for more than a half hour, while I performed like a contortionist all around it in order to see and sketch its delicately formed head from a variety of angles.

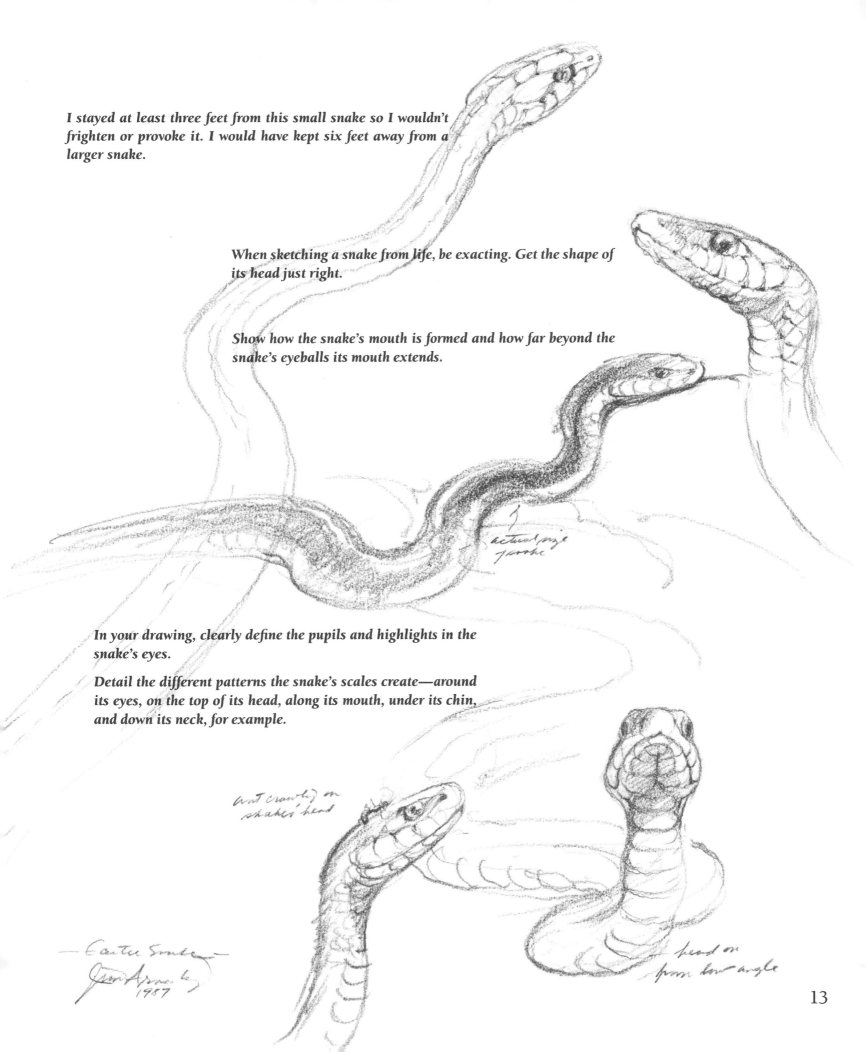

I stayed at least three feet from this small snake so I wouldn't frighten or provoke it. I would have kept six feet away from a larger snake.

When sketching a snake from life, be exacting. Get the shape of its head just right.

Show how the snake's mouth is formed and how far beyond the snake's eyeballs its mouth extends.

In your drawing, clearly define the pupils and highlights in the snake's eyes.

Detail the different patterns the snake's scales create—around its eyes, on the top of its head, along its mouth, under its chin, and down its neck, for example.

actual size garter

ant crawling on snakes' head

Garter Snake
Jim Arnosky
1987

head on from low angle

13

The birdbath is surrounded by a fragrant circle of herbs. Our herb garden is on a spot where a huge maple tree once stood. Long ago the tree was cut down and its stump burned. I chopped up the stump's charred and rotting remains, then plowed and tilled the ground around it. In that rich soil, Deanna planted parsley, sage, basil, thyme, chives, oregano, dill, and comfrey.

All the herbs thrive on the spot, especially the comfrey. It grows so thick and tall that we have to support its stalks with twine and wooden stakes.

I have discovered that the broader I make my pencil lines and the more impressionistically I apply shading, the closer I come to getting a lush green look in my sketches.

To make the comfrey's fuzzy and supple leaves look that way in my drawing, I let my shading lines slightly overlap the leaves' outlines.

After completing the overall shading on a plant or group of plants, use a sharpened point to add fine and dark details. Then, with a kneadable eraser, lift light-colored stems, leaves, and blossoms out of the gray areas.

Deanna's herb garden
July 2 1987

15

This cat we call Climber because, when he was a kitten, he used to climb up the outside of the screen door and peer into the house. Climber had been busy all morning hunting in the garden. Now he was napping on the porch.

Using a carpenter's pencil I had found in my toolbox, I dashed off this sketch. Climber was in a deep sleep. The noise of the pencil's extra-wide lead scratching on my drawing paper—a sound not unlike a mouse rustling in dry grasses—did not stir him.

Baby Catbird — three studies

July 3 1981

Meet the sole surviving baby catbird in the nest in our lilac bushes. Originally there were three nestlings. Two disappeared sometime during the last rains. I searched the ground below the nest but found no sign of them.

This bird, perched on the edge of the empty nest, chirps all day long. When one of its parents returns with food, the little bird hops excitedly into the air, opening wide its big yellow mouth to receive the morsel. As soon as it is left alone again, the bird begins chirping for more.

I began these sketches close by the nest, attempting to stay out of sight, but I was soon discovered. The bird stopped chirping, turned, and looked me squarely in the eyes. At one point, it opened its mouth as if I should drop some food into it.

Normally I do not sketch birds that are in their nests, for fear of disturbing them. But nothing seemed to faze this cocky little bird, and its parents were so busy trying to satisfy its insatiable hunger that they never noticed me.

We are having a drenching summer shower. On the far side of the pasture, the sheep are taking shelter under the evergreen trees. The whole scene appears dull and gray, except for the pond, which shines like liquid metal.

This sketch was done looking out of our kitchen window. I was under roof. The sheep were under boughs. Between us poured the rain.

I used the broad flat lead of the carpenter's pencil as I would a squared-off paintbrush, applying large areas of tones and "chiseling out" shapes.

To make my drawing look as gray and rainy as the actual scene, I rubbed my thumb on the paper, smearing every part of the sketch except the area of the pond's surface, which I wanted to look bright.

Shelter from the Storm
— Sheep on the far side of the pasture
standing under the evergreen boughs
during a downpour.
Jan Arnosky
July 14 1987

21

"Stump and Flowers" was sketched on a very hot, humid afternoon. It is impressionistic, after my hazy vision of the actual stump across the yard. I sat back on my stool and worked casually at the picture, applying broad strokes, short dashes, scribbles, squiggles, and spots—all representing the natural lines and shapes I was seeing. I was not concerned with realistically depicting anything.

Yet when I stood and walked a few yards away from my easel and viewed the sketch, the old stump with its loosened bark, patches of moss and lichen, and various flowers growing in, on, and around it, were all clearly there on the paper!

When you are sketching impressionistically, work quickly. Concentrate more on the natural lines, shapes, and shadows of your subject than on your sketch. Hide your eraser. There are no mistakes to be made. Do not evaluate your picture until you are finished.

23

This sketch shows a garden spot between the mowed lawn and a patch of tall grass. The lawn grass and the tall grass are the same type of grass. Only when permitted to grow wild and tall, and ultimately to seed, can grass plants be fully appreciated. Only then can you see them bend and sway and bow their heads in a breeze. Only then can you hear their long green blades swishing together.

Let an area of your lawn go unmowed so you can see what the grass looks like when it is fully grown.

There are always some plants in a garden that escape harvesting and grow to maturity. These plants become coarse, inedible, and I think more interesting to look at and to draw.

In this sketch there are two onions that have grown tall and are fully bloomed. The branchy plants with small oval leaves that you see just beyond the lettuce rows are radishes we neglected to pull.

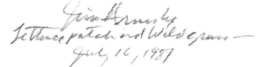

24

Every leaf has a stem or stalk. Even lettuce leaves, which appear to be leaf only, have stalks on which the leaves are formed. When you are aware of and can recognize the stem or stalk of every leaf you see, drawing leaves becomes much easier.

25

While I was working away at an enjoyable but seemingly endless sketch of a gnarled tree trunk and the surrounding brush on the leeward shore of a lake, a raven passed above me. I could hear its wings beating against the wind. Instinctively I added the bird's black form to my drawing exactly as I saw it through the tangle of leafy stems and branches. And suddenly the picture was complete.

I started sketching the greenery the way I first perceived it—as a chaos of lines, shapes, and shadows. Then, as my eyes focused on individual plants, I sketched their leaves, branches, and stems into the scene. Slowly the picture began to have a more detailed and orderly look.

27

On the hottest day of July, I sat out on the lawn under my umbrella and sketched the shady maple tree. I couldn't have seen the tree's shade as well if I had been sitting in it, though that was where I longed to be. It looked so cool there.

The sun's heat came through the fabric of my umbrella, cooked me under it, and made putty out of my kneadable eraser.

Before you begin a sketch, determine the angle from which you wish to view your subject. Then set your easel to accommodate your chosen vantage point—not vice versa.

Never give up entirely on a sketch done outdoors. This picture is only a portion of the larger sketch I actually did, most of which was drawn too dark and became badly smudged. However, this salvaged section has much to look at and enjoy.

In summer, wherever there is heavy foliage, shadows are deep and dark.

On July 19 I went to the pond behind our place to sketch in the cool drizzling rain. The pond rests in a wooded hollow. Its still water surface is darkened by the reflections of surrounding spruce trees. As I sketched, trout began to rise, and I added each rise ring to my drawing as it occurred.

A kingfisher swooped through the scene, chattering as it passed close to where I was sitting. The bird's white belly and underwings stood out against the dark green background. I must tell you, I sketched that kingfisher nearly as fast as it flew by!

31

At another pond, I came upon a multitude of frogs. There were over a hundred of them in various stages of metamorphosis. Some were still tadpoles. Most were fully developed frogs that still had their tadpole tails. During this time in a frog's life its tail is its only source of food and is gradually being absorbed into its body.

I turned to a fresh leaf in my drawing pad and sat right there among the frogs. They reacted by squeaking and climbing clumsily over one another in the inch-deep water. After a few minutes, they calmed back down. Close by was a huge bullfrog. It looked as if it was just waiting for one of the smaller frogs to hop near enough to be gobbled up.

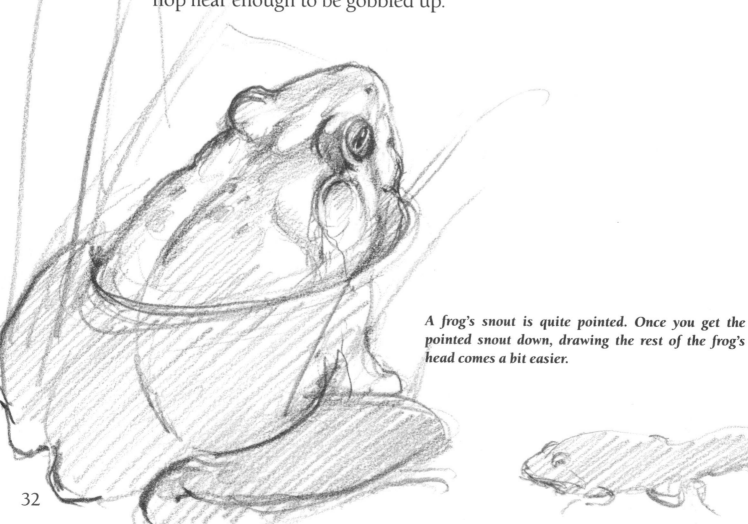

A frog's snout is quite pointed. Once you get the pointed snout down, drawing the rest of the frog's head comes a bit easier.

Frogs' "forearms" are thicker and more oval than their "upper arms."

Notice the way a frog folds its hind legs. It is this fold you must learn to draw in order to depict frogs accurately.

34

Here is a view of the barn and pasture as seen from Pickerel Cove, a small cup of wet land near the river. The cove is divided into sections by a number of little islands. Between these grassy spots, still pools of water reflect the world around.

The lush growth and cool clean water attract all kinds of wildlife. Here I have watched beaver, otter, moose, deer, geese, ducks, herons, hawks, and warblers of every color and stripe.

For quick landscapes, I establish a shorthand of various line strokes to suggest and distinguish different areas of water, land, and foliage. In this sketch I used vertical strokes for grass, brush, and background trees. Diagonal lines depict foreground growth and individual trees' leafy crowns. Horizontal lines were used only for water surfaces.

I carry a compact leather-jacketed sketch pad in one of the pockets of my fishing vest. The sketches on the next pages were made between casts for trout and bass.

The bullfrog was on a shoreline boulder. I waded close enough to see it clearly, but not so close as to make it jump, and sketched the frog twice. First, looking down on it—an odd and interesting angle. Then again, after the bullfrog turned away from me and faced the setting sun.

It was near dark in the forest where I stood doing this quick sketch of the eerie scene out on the lake. The rippling lake surface reflected and magnified the twilight. The air had turned quite cool, causing ghostly plumes of mist to rise off the warm water. Three bats had just begun their evening flight.

37

As I drew these morning glories on the bank of a trout stream, rain ran down the pad over my pencil lines. The whole sketch was being smeared, but I kept drawing anyway. See how nicely it dried!

Morning Glory
during an evening
rain shower.
Jim Arnosky
July 87

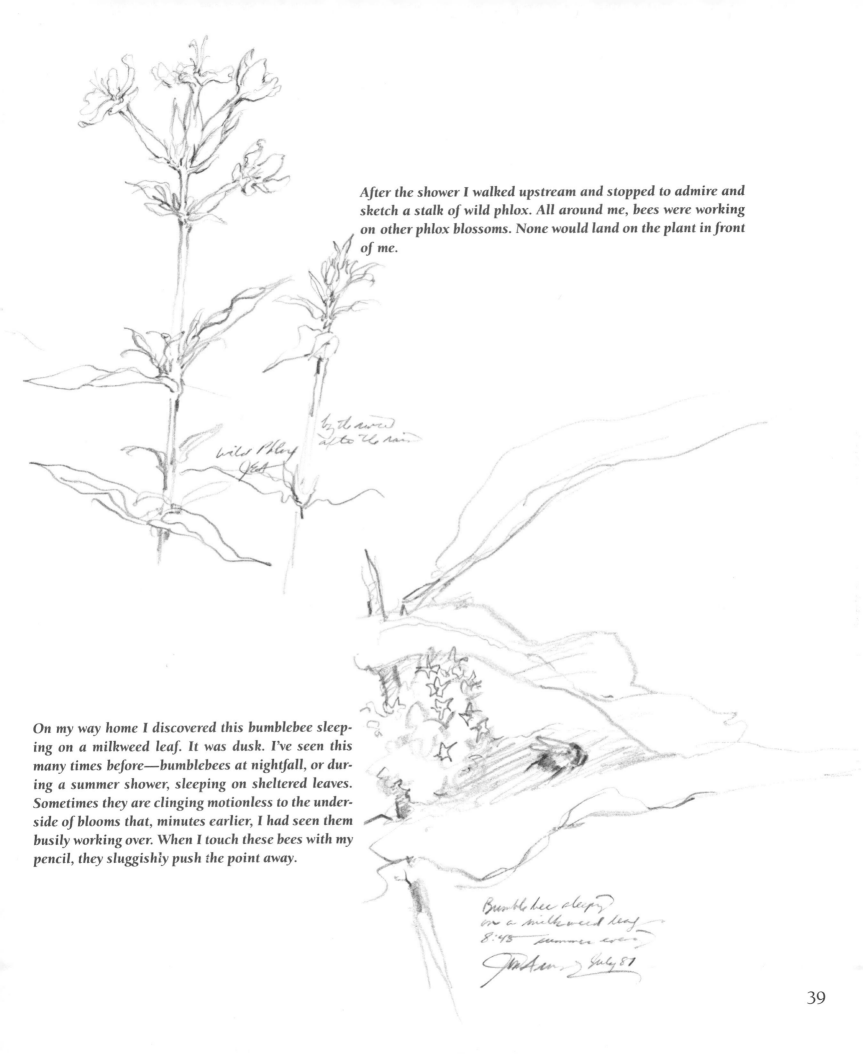

After the shower I walked upstream and stopped to admire and sketch a stalk of wild phlox. All around me, bees were working on other phlox blossoms. None would land on the plant in front of me.

wild Phlox
yea

by the river
after the rain

On my way home I discovered this bumblebee sleeping on a milkweed leaf. It was dusk. I've seen this many times before—bumblebees at nightfall, or during a summer shower, sleeping on sheltered leaves. Sometimes they are clinging motionless to the underside of blooms that, minutes earlier, I had seen them busily working over. When I touch these bees with my pencil, they sluggishly push the point away.

Bumble bee sleeping
on a milkweed leaf
8:45 summer eve
July 81

The brook trout below was caught on a fly, carefully unhooked, then gently placed in a two-gallon fishbowl. I had furnished the container with some stones and filled it with the trout's cold native water.

I was about to begin sketching my live model when suddenly rain started to come down hard. I left the trout in the bowl out in the pouring rain and took shelter inside my truck, which was parked nearby. As soon as the shower had passed, the sun came out in a brilliant blue sky. Golden light poured into the fishbowl. I sketched the captive trout as it appeared suspended in the sunlit water. When I was finished, I released the fish and watched it swim away.

Remember, a fish breathing in a small tank will deplete the oxygen in the water. Do not keep a fish captive for more than forty-five minutes without adding a fresh supply of water (and with it life-giving oxygen) to the tank.

These more detailed sketches were made last summer. They also were drawn from a living trout, which was caught on a fly, detained awhile in a glass container, then released.

I have noticed that the dark pupil of a fish's eye does not reflect light. Any highlight in a fish's eye will show up on the iris.

Brook Trout
from life-JEA

The turtle was crossing a dusty dirt road, going from a stream on one side to a pond on the other side. I walked up to the turtle and squatted on the road right in its way, rudely forcing it to yield to my curiosity as I sketched its shell design—something that fascinates me on every turtle I see.

I sketched two more views of the turtle hiding inside its shell. Then, since I had prolonged its trip under the midday sun to the cool comfort of the pond, I picked the traveler up and carried it there myself.

Notice the turtle's long claws, its pug nose, and the two dots it has for nostrils.

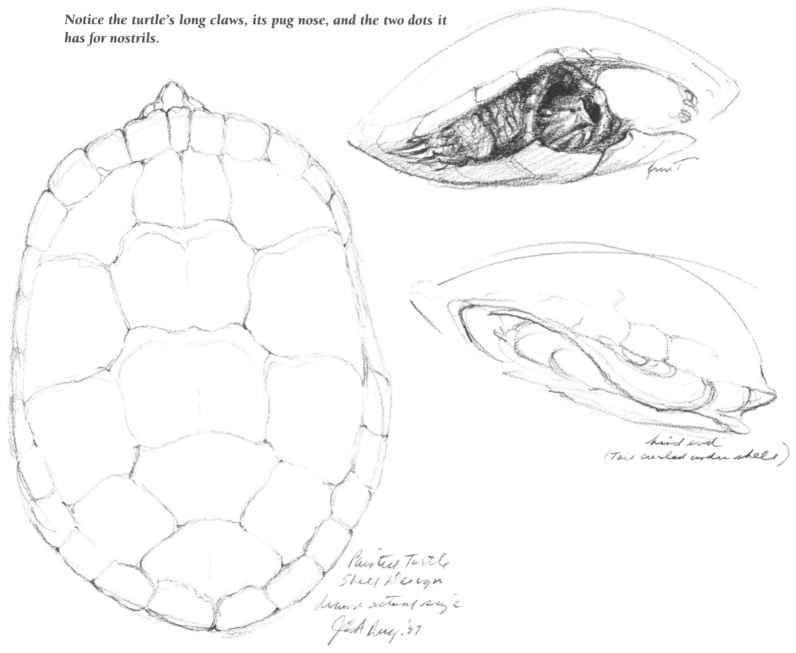

hind end
(Tail curled under shell)

Painted Turtle
Shell Design
drawn actual size
Josh Aug. '87

When a turtle walks, its legs rub up against its shell. The scales on the turtle's legs are thick and coarse to withstand this wear.

A turtle's head appears smooth and scaleless.

This is *Musquash,* my thirteen-year-old canoe. *Musquash* is forest green fiberglass outside and brown wood inside. She hides well. This summer I cached my canoe on the shore of a remote mountain pond. There, slipped under a low-hanging spruce bough, *Musquash* weathers the days and nights. Spiders have been making their webs under her gunwales. Squirrels perch on her overturned hull and strip spruce cones. Insects and mice are chewing designs in the old canoe's varnished decks.

Porcupines live around the pond. I expect a porcupine soon to discover the paddle stowed under the canoe and gnaw its handle for the salt left from the sweat of my hands.

When I made this sketch of *Musquash,* my hands were hot and sweaty and stiff from paddling more than a mile of shoreline.

Is there anything more shapely than a canoe?

When sketching a canoe, you have to be loving and exacting. Carefully copy the graceful curving lines of the gunwales. Show the slight bulge in the hull. Capture the upward sweep of the bow.

Make the thwart look firm in its place across the canoe's beam. Be sure the seats are constructed properly and look strong enough to sit on.

Master drawing canoes and you will be able to draw any other boat a person can build.

It's a good thing pencils can float. During the summer I spend a lot of time around, in, and on water. This is *Mayfly*. *Mayfly* is teaching me to sail. On a day too windy for a beginner to set sail, I did this sketch from *Mayfly*'s dinghy, which was bobbing like a cork on the water. The motion made it impossible to draw a straight line. Yet I believe this sketch captures the essence of its subject.

Because *Mayfly* has a broad beam and a full keel, she is a very stable vessel. I was relaxing in the cockpit when I decided to draw the lovely wooden daysailer that is moored next to us. In this instance the subject, not the artist, was in motion. As I drew, the little boat rocked with the waves. Its wooden mast beat back and forth like a metronome keeping time.

As a boat moves about on water, its shape appears to change with each new angle of view. Choose the angle you wish to sketch. Then, using very light lines, sketch the boat each time it assumes the angle that gives it the particular shape you are drawing.

Once you have the shape of the hull, add the decks. Then draw every detail of construction you can see.

When sketching a sailboat, it is important that you understand its rigging. Cables called stays support the mast fore and aft. Cables called shrouds support the mast port and starboard. On the mast there are lines called halyards that raise and lower the sails. If you can make sense of a boat's rigging, you will have less difficulty drawing it.

47

In time every season comes to an end. A chilly autumn wind
was blowing over the lake when I made this last sketch of
summer.